A Big Change

by Nancy Day
illustrated by Gary Krejca

PEARSON

Scott
Foresman

Editorial Offices: Glenview, Illinois • Parsippany, New Jersey • New York, New York
Sales Offices: Needham, Massachusetts • Duluth, Georgia • Glenview, Illinois
Coppell, Texas • Ontario, California • Mesa, Arizona

"It's not fair!" Jen stamped her foot. "I love the city. I don't want to move."

"I think you'll both enjoy the country when we get there," Dad said. "I'll take you fishing."

After dinner Jen and her brother
Roy went up to the roof. "I'll miss you,
Louie," Jen said to her pigeon.

"Bye, Lisa," Jen waved to her best friend. Tears ran down her cheeks.

As they drove away, they passed Jen's block, shops, her school, and the park. They crossed the bridge out of the city.

They passed fields with corn and cows. They came into a little town. They drove up a driveway to a little house.

"We're home!" Mom said. Jen kept quiet.

That afternoon Dad fixed things in the new house.

"Can we go fishing?" Jen asked.

"Not yet, but soon," said Dad.

The next morning, Jen went exploring. Roy joined her.

"What's that animal across the road?" Jen asked. They walked over.

Then they heard a chuckle. A strong looking girl popped out of a shed. "It's a goat!" she said. "And I'm Amelia."

"What are goats?" Roy asked.

"Goats are friendly animals," said Amelia. "They're no trouble."

Jen ran home to get her dad. They all went back to talk to Amelia. Soon, Jen was leading their new goat home.

"Let's call him Grazer," she told Roy.

That night, Dad said, "Let's go fishing tomorrow! We'll catch giant fish here."

"Yeah!" yelled Jen and Roy.

Jen smiled at Mom. "I think I like the country!" she said. Mom winked at her.

Migration

Have you seen birds fly south for the winter? We say they *migrate*. People can migrate too.

Sometimes people migrate, or move, to find jobs. Sometime they want to be in a new place. People may also migrate to warmer places in the winter. This could help them stay healthy. What are some other reasons you can think of that people might migrate?